AF407161

X-TRAORDINARY: A TURNER SYNDROME STORY

MCKENZIE BANKHEAD

X-TRAORDINARY: A TURNER SYNDROME STORY

Elyse Kasparian Webb

X-traordinary:
A Turner Syndrome Story

written by: McKenzie Bankhead

Illustrated by: Elyse Kasparian Webb

Everyone has a body.
Every body is different.

Some people
are tall. Some
people are
short.

Some people have
wavy hair.
Some people
have straight
hair.

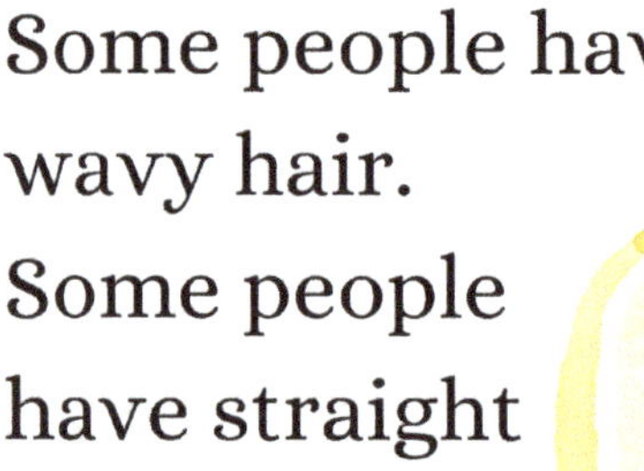

My name is Brooklyn. I'm
short with long, golden hair
and blue eyes.

I have Turner syndrome!

Bodies are made of special
building blocks.

When my body was made,
one X block was left out.

Most girls have two X blocks,
but I have one.

This is called Turner syndrome.

I get to see a lot of great doctors
to help me take care of my body.

The
endocrinologist
helps me grow.

The cardiologist
listens to
my heart.

The
ophthalmologist
checks my eyes.

My therapist and I talk
about my feelings.

Because I have Turner syndrome, I'll be shorter than most of my friends.

This makes me great at gymnastics.

What are you great at?

To help my body grow and my bones get strong, I get a growth hormone shot every day. I felt nervous at first, but my friend lion helps me be brave!

(I pick a new spot each day!)

My teachers at school say I'm great
at reading and spelling.

I'm organized and love doing art projects
and being creative!

When I grow up, I want to be an astronaut
and travel to Mars!

I also want to be a mom when I get older! It might be hard for my body to grow a baby, but there are lots of ways to have my own family.

I might adopt a baby.

I might be able to grow a baby myself with
my doctor's supervision.

Someone might be able to
grow the baby for me.

I know that having Turner syndrome is just one part of what makes me special.

I may be small, but I have big dreams and I know I can do anything I put my mind to.

You can too!